PROVOKING UNMERITED FAVOR

And I will give this people favour in the sight of the Egyptians: and it shall come to pass, that, when ye go, ye shall not go empty.

Exodus 3:21

by
Franklin N. Abazie

Provoking Unmerited Favor
COPYRIGHT 2016 BY Franklin N Abazie
ISBN: 978-1-94513314-5

All right reserved. This book or any portion thereof may not be reproduced or used in any manner whatsoever without the express written permission of the publisher, except for the use of brief quotations in a book review. All Bible quotes are from King James Version and others as noted.

Published by: F N ABAZIE PUBLISHING HOUSE—aka, Empowerment Bookstore

That I may publish with the voice of thanksgiving and tell of all thy wondrous works.
Psalms 26:7

To order additional copies, wholesales or booking call:
the Church office (973-372-7518)
or Empowerment Bookstore Hotline (973-393-8518)

Worship address:
343 Sanford Avenue, Newark, New Jersey 07106
Administrative Head Office address:
33 Schley Street Newark New Jersey 07112
Email: pastorfranknto@yahoo.com
Website www.fnabaziehealingministries.org
Publishing House: www.fnabaziepublishinghouse.org

This book is a production of F N Abazie Publishing House. A publication Arms of Miracle of God Ministries 2016.
First Edition

CONTENTS

THE MANDATE OF THE COMMISSION......................iv
ARMS OF THE COMMISSION..v
INTRODUCTION..vi
CHAPTER 1
The Supreme Nature of Favor................................1
CHAPTER 2
Sowing the Seeds of Favor.....................................11
CHAPTER 3
The Power of the Favor of God..............................14
CHAPTER 4
Prayer of Salvation..42
CHAPTER 5
About the Author...50

THE MANDATE OF THE COMMISSION

"The moment is due to impact your world through the revival of the healing & miracle ministry of Jesus Christ of Nazareth.

"I am sending you to restore health unto thee and I will heal thee of thy wounds, said the Lord of Host."

ARMS OF THE COMMISSION

1) F N Abazie Ministries—Miracle of God Ministries (Miracle Chapel Intl)

2) F N Abazie TV Ministries: Global Television Ministry Outreach

3) F N Abazie Radio Ministries: Radio Broadcasting Outreach

4) F N Abazie Publishing House: Book Publication

5) F N Abazie Bible School: also called Word of Healing Bible School (W.O.H.B.S.)

6) F N Abazie Evangelistic Ass: Miracle of God Ministries: Global Crusade

7) Empowerment Bookstore: Book distribution

8) F N Abazie Helping Hands: Meeting the Help of the Needy Worldwide

9) F N Abazie Disaster Recovery Mission: Global Disaster Recovery

10) F N Abazie Prison Ministry: Prison Ministry For All Convicts "Second Chance"

Some of our ministry arms are awaiting the appointed time to commence.

INTRODUCTION

In these last days everybody is in need of and desperate for the FAVOR OF GOD. Every time you meet a man/woman of FAVOR, it shows on him/her. FAVOR announces itself. The FAVOR OF GOD does not need any advertisement. THE FAVOR OF GOD promotes and advertises itself. In my understanding, we must all follow the footsteps of JESUS CHRIST. *"And Jesus increased in wisdom and stature, and in favour with God and man."* (Luke 2:52)

ASPIRE TO ACQUIRE
THE DESIRES YOU ADMIRE

In these last days full of struggles and assaults from the devil, we must all be FAVORED by MEN and by GOD. It is written of Samuel: *"And the child Samuel grew on, and was in favour both with the Lord, and also with men."* (1 Samuel 2:26) Over the years GOD'S FAVOR has been grossly misinterpreted and misrepresented.

In this publication, I'd love to shed some striking revelation concerning the FAVOR OF GOD. Every time GOD chooses a man to favor him/her, there is usually an argument by envious and jealous people around them.

Mary's husband Joseph was uncomfortable when out of FAVOR. GOD chose Mary to be conceived by the HOLY SPIRIT. *"And the angel came in unto her, and said, Hail, thou that art highly favoured, the Lord is with thee: blessed art thou among women."* (Luke 1:28) *"And the angel answered and said unto her, The Holy Ghost shall come upon thee, and the power of the Highest shall overshadow thee: therefore also that holy thing which shall be born of thee shall be called the Son of God."* (Luke 1:35)

FAVOR IS THE FLAVOR
THAT COLORS A MAN'S LABOR

It is written: *"Now God had brought Daniel into favour and tender love with the prince of the eunuchs."* (Daniel 1:9) Unless otherwise stated, it is GOD that prospers any man HE chooses. *"What man is he that feareth the Lord? him shall he teach in the way that he shall choose."* (Psalms 25:12)

FAVOR IS
THE PLATFORM FOR PROSPERITY

It is written: *"And the Lord gave the people favour in the sight of the Egyptians, so that they lent unto them such things as they required. And they spoiled the Egyptians."* (Exodus 12:36)

FAVOR IS THE PLATFORM
FOR THE ANNOINTING

Remember: *"And I will give this people favour in the*

sight of the Egyptians: and it shall come to pass, that, when ye go, ye shall not go empty." (Exodus 3:21)

The word FAVOR is a very familiar word. We get the word FAVORITE from this root word. The word favor as a noun is an attitude of approval or liking. It is an act of kindness beyond what is due or usual. This publication is a teaching that explains the insight on how to PROVOKE THE UNMERITED FAVOR OF GOD. It is written: *"In his favour is life."* (Psalms 30:5) It is my desire you ENCOUNTER the SUPERNATURAL FAVOR OF GOD. READ, MEDITATE, REFLECT AND BE BLESSED.

HAPPY READING!!

HOW DO I PROVOKE THE UNMERITED FAVOR OF GOD?

BY SHOWING FAVOR TO EVERY BODY AROUND US

The scriptures teach us that we must show favor to others if we are to receive the unmerited favor of GOD. *"He that diligently seeketh good procureth favour."* (Proverbs 11:27) We must show favor to everyone around us at all times, especially when it is in the power of our hand to do so. If we must receive the unmerited favor of God, we must practice showing kindness and favor to all and at all times. *"Withhold not good from them to whom it is due, when it is in the power of thine hand to do it. Say not unto thy neighbour, Go, and come again, and tomorrow I will give; when thou hast it by thee."* (Proverbs 3:27-28) Remember, it's a sin if you willingly refuse to show kindness and favor to others when you are in the position to do so.

> *Therefore to him that knoweth to do good,*
> *and doeth it not, to him it is sin.*
> **James 4:17**

BY PRAYING THROUGH THE PROMISES OF THE ALMIGHTY GOD

I have always AGREED on the mysteries of provoking the favor of God by praying through the promises of God. We must all stand at the altar of prayer if we desire to activate the unmerited favor of GOD. It is written: *"He shall pray unto God, and he will be favourable unto him: and he shall see his face with joy: for he will render unto man his righteousness."* (Job 33:26)

BY OBEYING THE COMMANDMENT OF GOD

As long as we are living in disobedience, we are not qualified for the unmerited favor of GOD. The Bible made it crystal clear: *"If ye be willing and obedient, ye shall eat the good of the land: But if ye refuse and rebel, ye shall be devoured with the sword: for the mouth of the Lord hath spoken it."* (Isaiah 1:19-20) Remember: *"My son, forget not my law; but let thine heart keep my commandments: For length of days, and long life, and peace, shall they add to thee. Let not mercy and truth forsake thee: bind them about thy neck; write them upon the table of thine heart: So shalt thou find favour and good understanding in the sight of God and man."* (Proverbs 3:1-4)

BY UNDERSTANDING GOD'S WISDOM

God's wisdom is the super wisdom that guarantees wealth and health. This wisdom is creative and innovative in its multi-dimension. Every time we locate God's wisdom in print, the unmerited favor of God follows us in our lives. Talking about understanding God's wisdom, the Bible says: *"For whoso findeth me findeth life, and shall obtain favour of the Lord."* (Proverbs 8:35)

BY LIVING A RIGHTEOUS LIFESTYLE

As long as we are living a righteous lifestyle, God is committed to showing us favor in our lives. But if we continue in our evil, wicked ways, bad luck and trouble is bound to show up in our lives. *"Fools make a mock at sin: but among the righteous there is favour."* (Proverbs 14:9) It is written: *"But it shall not be well with the wicked, neither shall he prolong his days, which are as a shadow; because he feareth not before God."* (Ecclesiastes 8:13)

BY DEVELOPING A GOOD UNDERSTANDING IN ALL THINGS

The word of the Lord is the access key to life. Every time you have the access key, you open any closed door. Until there is clarity and understanding of the scriptures, every good thing in life is not guaranteed for us. *"Good understanding giveth favour: but the way of transgressors is hard."* (Proverbs 13:15)

We must understand the word of God if we must become partakers of His divine nature. *"Whereby are given unto us exceeding great and precious promises: that by these ye might be partakers of the divine nature, having escaped the corruption that is in the world through lust."* (2 Peter 1:4)

BY THE UNDERSTANDING THE WISDOM OF GOD

The wisdom of God is the custodian of wealth. A man once said that wealth is your ability to think. In my opinion, divine wisdom is the platform for all impactful wealth anywhere in the world. With reference to the divine wisdom of God, the Bible says: *"For whoso findeth me findeth life, and shall obtain favour of the Lord."* (Proverbs 8:35) It is written: *"For wisdom is better than rubies; and all the things that may be desired are not to be compared to it. I wisdom dwell with prudence, and find out knowledge of witty inventions."* (Proverbs 8:11-12)

And I will give this people favour in the sight of the Egyptians: and it shall come to pass, that, when ye go, ye shall not go empty.
Exodus 3:21

*HIS DESTINY WAS
THE CROSS....*

*HIS PURPOSE WAS
LOVE....*

*HIS REASON WAS
YOU....*

HOW TO POSITION OURSELVES FOR THE FAVOR OF GOD

REPENT

We must always understand what it means to repent of our sins. Unless you repent, you do not stand a chance to get God's favor in life. Repentance is always the key to deliverance and the first step into Healing and all forms of Restoration in life. Peter replied to a question from the crowd "what shall we do?" with: *"Repent and be baptized every one of you, in the name of Jesus Christ for the forgiveness of your sins. And you will receive the gift of the Holy Spirit."* (Acts 2:38)

It is scripturally established that it shall not be well with the wicked. We must therefore repent of all our wicked ways in life if we are to become candidates of His supernatural favor in life. *"If my people, which are called by my name, shall humble themselves, and pray, and seek my face, and turn from their wicked ways; then will I hear from heaven, and will forgive their sin, and will heal their land."* (2 Chronicles 7:14)

FAITH

But without faith it is impossible to please him: for he that cometh to God must believe that he is, and that he is a rewarder of them that diligently seek him.
Hebrews 11:6

Most people forget that God is spirit. As long

as we please him with our faith, God is obligated to return the favor into our lives. It is written: *"When a man's ways please the Lord, he maketh even his enemies to be at peace with him."* (Proverbs 16:7) *"And Jesus answering saith unto them, Have faith in God."* (Mark 11:2)

DECISION & WILL POWER

So many of us sing this popular church song: *"I Have Decided to Follow Jesus,"* but really we do not activate the appropriate action necessary for the favor of God to manifest upon our ways. *"And why call ye me, Lord, Lord, and do not the things which I say?"* (Luke 6:46)

So many of us struggle with hardship and difficulties in life as a result of lack of divine help from God. *"Let us therefore come boldly unto the throne of grace, that we may obtain mercy, and find grace to help in time of need."* (Hebrews 4:16) It is written: *"Except the Lord build the house, they labour in vain that build it: except the Lord keep the city, the watchman waketh but in vain. It is vain for you to rise up early, to sit up late, to eat the bread of sorrows: for so he giveth his beloved sleep."* (Psalms 127:1-2) Decision as the wheel of life takes us to our desired destination—either into HEAVEN or into HELL.

We must make a decision to live for Jesus Christ. Have you made plans to make heaven at last?

PRAYER

And he spake a parable unto them to this end,
that men ought always to pray, and not to faint.
Luke 18:1

Without a prayer lifestyle, we do not stand a chance as a spiritual people to obtain help from above. *"I will lift up mine eyes unto the hills, from whence cometh my help. My help cometh from the Lord, which made heaven and earth. He will not suffer thy foot to be moved: he that keepeth thee will not slumber. Behold, he that keepeth Israel shall neither slumber nor sleep. The Lord is thy keeper: the Lord is thy shade upon thy right hand. The sun shall not smite thee by day, nor the moon by night. The Lord shall preserve thee from all evil: he shall preserve thy soul. The Lord shall preserve thy going out and thy coming in from this time forth, and even for evermore."* (Psalms 121:1-8)

Prayer is a channel to connect to God's favor. Every time we pray, God looks into our circumstance and grants us the desired answer for our prevailing petition. Every answered petition from God is because of God's supernatural favor upon our lives. It is written: *"For the Lord God is a sun and shield: the Lord will give grace and glory: no good thing will he withhold from them that walk uprightly."* (Psalms 84:11)

PRAYER POINT TO ACTIVATE
THE FAVOR OF GOD

1) Supernatural hand of God, surprise me with favor.

2) Spirit of God, switch my labor by your favor, in the name of Jesus.

3) Merciful Father, arranage your supernatural favor on my behalf, in the mighty name of Jesus.

4) Holy spirit, revive my life with your favor, in the mighty name of Jesus.

5) Power of God, dominate my life, in the mighty name of Jesus.

6) Hand of God, empower me to obstain help from man, in the mighty name of Jesus.

7) Fire of God, take control over my spiritual life, in the mighty name of Jesus.

8) I pronounce the supernatural favor of God over my life.

9) I destroy every root of sin in my life, in the mighty name of Jesus.

10) Sin shall not dominate my life, in the mighty name

of Jesus.

11) Father lord, destroy every tortise spirit over my life, in the mighty name of Jesus.

12) Spirit of God, revive your power over my life, in the mighty name of Jesus.

13) Power of God, hijack my harassers, in the mighty name of Jesus.

14) Blood of Jesus, favor my life.

15) Lord, baptize me with youir power, in the name of Jesus

16) Holy ghost, fire breath upon me in a new dimension of a higher order.

17) Power of God, possess and take control over my destiny, in the mighty name of Jesus.

18) Holy spirit, show me favor in the land of the living.

19) Spirit of God, destory all traps set against me, in the mighty name of Jesus.

20) I must be in favor, in the mighty name of Jesus.

21) I crush all demonic coffins watching and attacking

my destiny, in the mighty name of Jesus.

22) I must be blessed beyond my family members.

23) I must be blessed beyond my community.

24) I must become a blessing to my nation.

25) I must be blessed to bless my world.

CHAPTER 1

THE SUPREME NATURE OF FAVOR

For they got not the land in possession by their own sword, neither did their own arm save them: but thy right hand, and thine arm, and the light of thy countenance, because thou hadst a favour unto them.
Psalms 44:3

The word favor is an attitude of approval or liking. It is an act of kindness beyond what is due or usual—although man has failed to recognize and appreciate the favor of God in its infinite dimensions and appearance. God is more willing to not only show us His favor, but to also help our infirmities by His favor. *"Having therefore obtained help of God, I continue unto this day."* (Acts 26:22)

"For the Lord God is a sun and shield: the Lord will give grace and glory: no good thing will he withhold from them that walk uprightly." (Psalms 84:11)

It has always being the desire of GOD Almighty to show us favor from the days of Adam and Eve. It is written: *"For God so loved the world, that he gave his only begotten Son, that whosoever believeth in him should not perish, but have everlasting life."* (John 3:16)

Oftentimes in life God shows us so much favor that we neglect and ignore. We move on with our daily routine like nothing good has happened to us. *"For thou, Lord, wilt bless the righteous; with favour wilt thou compass him as with a shield."* (Psalms 5:12) God's favor is the reason for our whole existence. God's favor cannot be defined nor be measured in the weight of balance. God's favor is life: *"In his favour is life."* (Psalms 30:5)

WHAT IS THE FAVOR OF GOD?

The word "favor" is an attitude of approval or liking. It is an act of kindness beyond what is due or usual. *"For God so loved the world that he gave his only begotten Son, that whosoever believeth in him should not perish, but have everlasting life."* (John 3:16) The favor of God upon any man/woman is the anointing of God upon that person. This anointing protects, delivers and makes any man/woman with God's favor succeed and prevail against all of life's challenges. *"And when he had removed him, he raised up unto them David to be their king; to whom also he gave their testimony, and said, I have found David the son of Jesse, a man after mine own heart, which shall fulfil all my will."* (Acts 13:22)

We easily receive favor from people who show us favor in life. In the same manner, God shows us favor based on our righteousness and lifestyle. *"For the eyes of the LORD run to and fro throughout the whole earth, to show himself strong on behalf of them whose heart is perfect toward him."* (2 Chronicles 16:9) To be "perfect" towards Him means to obey His commandment and follow His statue, to seek His favor more than we seek the favor of any man. It is written: *"But Noah found grace in the eyes of the Lord."* (Genesis 6:8)

God seeks out those who love Him and love His commands so that He can bless, guide and protect them. (See Psalms 37:23 and Proverbs 3:5–6.) This does not mean that everyone who is prosperous or healthy has found favor with God. (See Jeremiah 12:1, Psalms 37:7 and Psalms 73:16.) Nor does it mean that those whom the Lord favors will never suffer difficulties. Many Bible characters had the Lord's favor, but also suffered great hardship in their lives. (See 2 Corinthians 6:4, Acts 14:22, Acts 20:23 and 1 Peter 2:19.)

Great men like Noah, who was moved with fear at some point in his life, found favor before God. (Genesis 6:8) Powerful prophets like Moses, who refused to be called Pharaoh's daughter's son and chose to suffer affliction with his fellow citizens, was a wanderer for 40 years until later finding favor before God. *"Now therefore, I pray thee, if I have found grace in thy sight, shew me now thy way, that I may know thee, that I may find grace in thy sight: and consider that this nation is thy people. And he said, My presence shall go with thee, and I will give thee rest."* (Exodus 33:14-15)

How about the man with an excellent spirit called Daniel, who witnessed four sitting presidents come and go? *"Now God had brought Daniel into favour and tender love with the prince of the eunuchs."* (Daniel 1:9) How about Mary, the special virgin chosen to be the mother of Jesus? *"And the angel came in unto her, and said, Hail, thou that art highly favoured, the Lord is with thee: blessed art thou among women. And when she saw him, she was troubled at his saying, and cast in her mind what manner of salutation this should be. And the angel said unto her, Fear not, Mary: for thou hast found favour with God. And, behold, thou shalt conceive in thy womb, and bring forth a son, and shalt call his name Jesus."* (Luke 1:28-31)

All these Biblical characters found favor before God, although they had their shortcomings and challenges in life. *"Those who are favored of God, recognize that nothing bad can over take their lives, besides God's good plan and purpose."* (Jeremiah 29:11) In addition to the manifestation of God favor, God's favor can be felt in the spirit. When we have the favor of the Lord, we rest in quiet confidence that our sins are forgiven (Romans 4:7), we are within the plan of God (Psalms 86:11) and that He is there for us at all times. (Isaiah 41:10, Matthew 28:20)

We are commanded to seek the Lord's favor. (Psalms 119:58, 2 Kings 13:4, Jeremiah 26:19, Zephaniah 2:3) *"When we seek His favor, we humble our hearts before Him."* (2 Kings 22:19) *"Seek Him for the kingdom of God and His righteousness, not just for the good things he will give us."* (Jeremiah 29:13)

One way to obtain favor from the Lord is to seek and understand the wisdom of God upon our own lives Proverbs 8:35 says, *"For those who find me [wisdom] find life and receive favor from the LORD."* Psalms 5:12 says, *"For thou, Lord, wilt bless the righteous; with favour wilt thou compass him as with a shield."* Finding favor with the Lord keeps our lives and thoughts pure because we desire to please Him more than we desire to please ourselves.

It is written: *"By faith Moses, when he was come to years, refused to be called the son of Pharaoh's daughter; Choosing rather to suffer affliction with the people of God, than to enjoy the pleasures of sin for a season; Esteeming the reproach of Christ greater riches than the treasures in Egypt: for he had respect unto the recompence of the reward. By faith he forsook Egypt, not fearing the wrath of the king: for he endured, as seeing him who is invisible."* (Hebrews 11:24-27) Until we are willing to pay the price of favor, we will never obtain the prize of the favor of God.

BIBLICAL CHARACTERS WHO OBTAINED THE FAVOR OF GOD

PAUL

Apostle Paul was a man who was greatly favored by God. *"For I am the least of the apostles, that am not meet to be called an apostle, because I persecuted the church of God. But by the grace of God I am what I am: and his grace which was bestowed upon me was not in vain; but I laboured more abundantly than they all: yet not I, but the grace of God which was with me."* (1 Corinthians 15:9-10) Apostle Paul was the greatest apostle that ever lived, not because he merited it, but because God selected him and favored him just like David.

RUTH

Ruth asked for and found FAVOR with Boaz

(Ruth 2:4) and became the great-grandmother of King David.

DAVID

"I have found David my servant; with my holy oil have I anointed him: With whom my hand shall be established: mine arm also shall strengthen him. The enemy shall not exact upon him; nor the son of wickedness afflict him. And I will beat down his foes before his face, and plague them that hate him. But my faithfulness and my mercy shall be with him: and in my name shall his horn be exalted." (Psalms 89:20-24) David made so much of an impact in his day because of the supernatural favor of God that was evident in his life. David found FAVOR with Saul (1 Samuel 16:22) and with God (Psalms 30:7). Despite his failings, God refers to David as *"a man after my own heart."* (Acts 13:22)

ESTHER

Esther became a celebrity because of the favor of God upon her life. (Esther 5:2) It was the favor that delivered Mordecai from the death.

MARY

It is written of Mary: *"To a virgin espoused to a man whose name was Joseph, of the house of David; and the virgin's name was Mary. And the angel came in unto her, and said, Hail, thou that art highly favoured, the Lord is with thee: blessed art thou among women. And when she saw him, she was troubled at his saying, and cast in her mind what manner of salutation this should be. And the angel said unto her, Fear not, Mary: for thou hast found favour with God. And, behold, thou shalt conceive in thy womb, and bring forth a son, and shalt call his name Jesus."* (Luke 1:27-31) Mary found favor before God.

JOSEPH

Joseph suffered so much affliction in his lifetime. But because of the favor of God upon his life, he was always honored and exonerated from all the accusations, assaults and difficulties. *"But the Lord was with Joseph, and shewed him mercy, and gave him favour in the sight of the keeper of the prison."* (Genesis 39:21)

JESUS

Even from conception, Jesus Christ was a much-favored child. He was God's choice for the redemption of man. *"It is written He that spared not his own Son, but delivered him up for us all, how shall he not with him also freely give us all things?"* (Romans 8:32) *"And Jesus increased in wisdom and stature, and in favour with God and man."* (Luke 2:52)

SUMMARY OF CHAPTER ONE

—The supreme nature of the favor of God is that it is higher than labor.

— God's favor is the flavor that colors a man's labor.

—We must all seek the favor of God in our lifetime.

— We must provoke the favor of God by showing favor to other people around us.

—We must provoke the favor of God by praying through the promises.

—We must provoke the promises of God by obeying the commandment of Jesus.

—If we must survive in this end time, we must search out all possible avenues to provoke the supernatural favor of God.

DECISION KEYS

1) Nothing changes until you make up your mind.

2) Decision is the gateway to deliverance.

3) Until you decide, no one will decide for you.

4) Your prosperity is proportional to your decisions.

5) The decision you make will determine the future you will create

6) Decision creates future and fulfills destinies.

7) Decision beautifies our future.

8) Decision keeps you out of trouble.

9) Decision exempts you from evil.

10) Decision guarantees eternity.

11) You can only go far in life by your faith decisions.

12) You are poor because you made such decisions.

13) Make a decision and change your life.

14) Life-changing decisions are a function of quality information.

15) Success in life is a function of decision.

16) Life experiences are full of decisions.

17) Decisions change destinies.

18) Never settle for information—always look for revelation.

19) You are where you are today based on your last decision.

20) Information is crucial in decision-making.

21) Decision-makers rule the world.

22) You can rule your world with quality decisions.

23) As long as you decide rightly, Satan cannot harrass you.

CHAPTER 2

SOWING THE SEEDS OF FAVOR

He that diligently seeketh good procureth favour.
Proverbs 11:27

Favor is a seed we must sow if we desire the favor of God in return into our life. I have witness a few selfish men and women seek for the favor of others, while they are not willing to show no body favor. In my own understanding favor is a seed we must sow and nurture in our life time.If you are selfish and does not give to others, you should not expect the favor of God from anyone.

For he that soweth to his flesh shall of the flesh reap corruption; but he that soweth to the Spirit shall of the Spirit reap life everlasting. And let us not be weary in well doing: for in due season we shall reap, if we faint not. As we have therefore opportunity, let us do good unto all men, especially unto them who are of the household of faith.
Galatians 6:8-10

In our life time we must always sow the seed of favor to all around us. It is inevitable to stop the seed of favor from growing. The seed of righteousness returns favor in life. "But Noah found grace in the eyes of the Lord" genesis6:8.

A carefull examination of the beatitudes in Mathew five from verse two will help our understanding:

And he opened his mouth, and taught them, saying, Blessed are the poor in spirit: for theirs is the kingdom of heaven. Blessed are they that mourn: for they shall be comforted. Blessed are the meek: for they shall inherit the earth. Blessed are they which do hunger and thirst after righteousness: for they shall be filled. Blessed are the merciful: for they shall obtain mercy. Blessed are the pure in heart: for they shall see God. Blessed are the peacemakers: for they shall be called the children of God. Blessed are they which are persecuted for righteousness' sake: for theirs is the kingdom of heaven. Blessed are ye, when men shall revile you, and persecute you, and shall say all manner of evil against you falsely, for my sake. Rejoice, and be exceeding glad: for great is your reward in heaven: for so persecuted they the prophets which were before you.
Matthew 5:2

THE BENEFITS OF GOD FAVOR

GOD'S FAVOR GRANTS US SUPERNATURAL INCREASES AND INEXPLICABLE PROMOTION

GOD'S FAVOR IS THE GATEWAY FOR RESTORATION TO ALL OUR INHERITANCE.

GOD'S FAVOR HONORS US IN THE MIDST OF PREVAILING ADVASARIES.

GOD'S FAVOR GUARANTEES SUPERNATURAL PROTECTION AGAINST OUR ASSETS AND LIVES.

GOD'S FAVOR BRINGS US INTO PROMINENCE AND RELEASES PREFERENTIAL TREATMENTS AND GLOBAL RECOGNITION.

CHAPTER 3

THE POWER OF THE FAVOR OF GOD

And Jesus increased in wisdom and stature, and in favour with God and man.
Luke 2:52

In my understanding, just one favor from the Lord will erase our lifetime labor. It is written: *"Labour not to be rich: cease from thine own wisdom."* (Proverbs 23:5) In these difficult times we live in, we must always seek out for the favor of God. *"What shall we then say to these things? If God be for us, who can be against us?"* (Romans 8:31)

Although everyone desires the favor of God in their life, we must always remember that the favor of God is not free of charge. There is a price to pay. Therefore we must be willing to do what provokes the favor of God. A lot of us seek the favor of a man, especially if they are in a position to help us in life. I have witnessed a situation where a man of high position was given a Porsche as a birthday present just because the giver was seeking a contract through the signature of this high profile CEO celebrating his birthday. The same is said of God—if you please God well, God will put you on His payroll. The Bible says, *"When a man way pleases the Lord, he maketh his enemies to be at peace with him."* (Proverbs 16:7)

If we must provoke the favor of God, we must activate our prayer life. The lifestyle of prayer is a fertile ground to receive the supernatural favor of God. *"Always labouring fervently for you in prayers, that ye may stand perfect and complete in all the will of God."* (Colossians 4:12) We must not only give attention to prayer, but we must always practice what we have learned from the Holy Bible. But to provoke the favor of God is not free. We must pay the price before we can be entitled to the supernatural favor of God.

And the child Samuel grew on, and was in favour both with the Lord, and also with men.
1 Samuel 2:26

Most of us labor for the things that perish in life. We are told by the Holy Bible: *"But lay up for yourselves treasures in heaven, where neither moth nor rust doth corrupt, and where thieves do not break through nor steal: For where your treasure is, there will your heart be also."* (Matthew 6:20-21)

Concerning the power of the favor of God, I am a living witness. If God chooses to favor you, it will be undeniable before all men. The favor of God exalts, it comes with honor, fame and all the riches this world can offer. When God remembered King Solomon, his entire life changed dramatically. Even Joseph the dreamer. Recall that God remembered Joseph his entire life.

CONDITIONS FOR THE FAVOR OF GOD

SOWING THE SEEDS OF FAVOR

We must sow favor as a seed if we are to receive favor in return in this life. *"For he that soweth to his flesh shall of the flesh reap corruption; but he that soweth to the Spirit shall of the Spirit reap life everlasting. And let us not be weary in well doing: for in due season we shall reap, if we faint not."* (Galatians 6:8-9)

LOVE EVERY ONE AROUND YOU

Love does not forget—as long as you can be loving to all around you. You will definitely reap love in return. *"Love is patient, love is kind. It does not envy, it does not boast, it is not proud. It does not dishonor others, it is not self-seeking, it is not easily angered, it keeps no record of wrongs. Love does not delight in evil but rejoices with the truth. It always protects, always trusts, always hopes, always perseveres."* (1 Corinthians 13:4-7)

If you sow love as a seed, God is obligated to favor your life. Jesus replied: *"Love the Lord thy God with all thy heart, and with all thy soul, and with all thy mind. This is the first and greatest commandment. And the second is like unto it, Thou shalt love thy neighbor as thyself."* (Matthew 22:37-39) As long as everyone around knows you as a loving personality, God will use one person among all to favor you within your lifetime.

WALK IN AGREEMENT WITH THE HOLY SPIRIT

We must be in agreement with the Holy Spirit if we must receive the favor of God from above. It is written: *"God is spirit, and his worshipers must worship in the Spirit and in truth."* (John 4:24) We must take advantage of the Holy Spirit by walking in communion and agreement and in fellowship with him. Remember: *"Again I say unto you, That if two of you shall agree on earth as touching anything that they shall ask, it shall be done for them of my Father which is in heaven."* (Matthew 18:19) *"Can two walk together, except they both agreed?"* (Amos 3:3)

THE RESULT OF THE FAVOR OF GOD

And the Lord gave the people favour in the sight of the Egyptians, so that they lent unto them such things as they required. And they spoiled the Egyptians.
Exodus 12:36

One of the greatest things that can happen to anyone is accessing the favor of God. King Saul was afraid of David because of the favor of God upon his life. *"And Saul was afraid of David, because the Lord was with him, and was departed from Saul."* (1 Samuel 18:12) It was the favor of God that took Joseph from the prison into the prime minister of Egypt. It was the same favor of God that brought David into the palace.

Remember…

King Herold feared John the Baptist because of the favor of God upon his life. *"For Herod feared John, knowing that he was a just man and an holy, and observed him; and when he heard him, he did many things, and heard him gladly."* (Mark 6:20)

SUMMARY OF CHAPTER 3

— We must seek God's favor by favoring others around us.

—The favor of God requires a liberal and cheerful giving heart.

— The favor of God terminates all struggles in life.

—The favor of God is unstoppable in its supply.

— The favor of God will protect and deliver us from trouble.

—The favor of God manifests naturally.

CANDIDATES FOR THE SUPERNATURAL FAVOR OF GOD

THE MEEK & THE HUMBLE

The seed of meekness generates the reward of meekness. *"Blessed are the merciful: for they shall obtain mercy."* (Matthew 5:7) As long as we have a humbled heart, God is ever willing to show us his favor. *"But he giveth more grace. Wherefore he saith, God resisteth the proud, but giveth grace unto the humble. Submit yourselves therefore to God. Resist the devil, and he will flee from you."* (James 4:6-7) God is seeking for a meek and humble heart to manifest his supernatural favor. *"Better it is to be of an humble spirit with the lowly, than to divide the spoil with the proud."* (Proverbs 16:19) I admonish you today to go all out to seek the favor of God by cultivating the spirit of meekness in the mighty name of Jesus.

THE RIGHTEOUS

It is written of Abraham: *"And he believed in the Lord; and he counted it to him for righteousness."* (Genesis 15:6) Every time we prove our righteousness before Him, we provoke His supernatural favor upon our lives. Righteousness is a kingdom secret for provoking the supernatural favor of God. For example, the word says: *"And who is he that will harm you, if ye be followers of that which is good?"* (1 Peter 3:13) We cannot practice righteousness and be rewarded with evil. It is impossible for the devil to assault us, especially when we have a clean heart and our hands are clean from the appearance of evil. I admonish you to come out of sin and seek the righteous way of life as commanded by the Holy Bible.

THE FAITHFUL

God is always looking for the faithful to reward them with favor in life. It is written of the faithful man: *"Faithful man shall abound with blessings: but he that maketh haste to be rich shall not be innocent."* (Proverbs 28:20) Remember: *"Faithful is he that calleth you, who also will do it."* (1 Thessalonians 5:24)

We must have faith in any little thing God has given us the privilege to have. *"His lord said unto him, Well done, good and faithful servant; thou hast been faithful over a few things, I will make thee ruler over many things: enter thou into the joy of thy lord."* (Matthew 25:23)

HINDRANCES TO THE FAVOR OF GOD

WICKEDNESS

Every woman/man of wickedness is a man/woman who is out of touch with the favor of God. It is a spiritual law that every time we behave wickedly, we are always entitled to receive wickedness in return in life. Wickedness is evil and evil must always bow before the good. *"The evil bow before the good; and the wicked at the gates of the righteous."* (Proverbs 14:19) It is written: *"Be not overcome of evil, but overcome evil with good."* (Romans 12:21)

Remember...

God is always angry at the wicked every day. *"God judgeth the righteous, and God is angry with the wicked every day."* (Psalms 7:11) Wickedness does not pay, neither is there a good return for doing evil. *"The wicked shall see it, and be grieved; he shall gnash with his teeth, and melt away: the desire of the wicked shall perish."* (Pslams 112:10) I admonish you to repent of any wicked doing and seek the favor of the Lord over your life.

BITTERNESS

The favor of God cannot co-habit with any form of bitterness in our heart. As long as our heart is bitter, God will withhold his favor from manifesting upon our lives. *"Looking diligently lest any man fail of the grace of God; lest any root of bitterness springing up trouble you, and thereby many be defiled."* (Hebrews 12:15) I admonish you to destroy every reservation of bitterness in your heart and seek the Lord's righteousness.

INIQUITY

The constant repetition of sin is what we call "iniquity." This means that every time we sin, we confess it and we go back again and sin once more. And as far as I know, only dogs return to their vomit. If we must provoke the favor of God, we must repent and stop going back to the sin that easily besets us. *"If I regard iniquity in my heart, the Lord will not hear me: But verily God hath heard me; he hath attended to the voice of my prayer."* (Psalms 66:18-19) God said: *"For I will forgive their iniquity, and I will remember their sin no more."* (Jeremiah 31:34)

Remember…..

> *But your iniquities have separated between you and your God, and your sins have hid his face from you, that he will not hear.*
> **Isaiah 59:2**

UN-FORGIVENESS

We cannot provoke the favor of God as long as we have un-forgiveness in our heart. *"Therefore if thou bring thy gift to the altar, and there rememberest that thy brother hath ought against thee; Leave there thy gift before the altar, and go thy way; first be reconciled to thy brother, and then come and offer thy gift."* (Matthew 5:23-24)

REGRET

Regret is an opening of the devil to hinder the supernatural favor of God from flowing into our lives. I read somewhere that "when you are depressed, you are living in the past, when you are anxious you are living in the future, but when you are at PEACE you are living in the present." Remember: *"Ye not the former things, neither consider the things of old. Behold, I will do a new thing; now it shall spring forth; shall ye not know it? I will even make a way in the wilderness, and rivers in the desert."* (Isaiah 43:18-19) If we must provoke the favor of God, we must accept our present condition with joy and delight. We must cherish every little happening

God has given us the previlege to witness in life. I admonish you, what has already happened we know and have seen. But what *would have* happened, we do not know. We must give God thanks for all things in life.

ACCESS TO RECEIVE THE PERSON OF THE HOLY SPIRIT

BE BORN AGAIN

It is commanded we must be born again. The holy Spirit is in charge of distributing the favor of God. Unless we have access through new birth, we cannot obtain the supernatural favor of God in our lives. *We must be born again.*

Jesus answered and said unto him, Verily, verily, I say unto thee, Except a man be born again, he cannot see the kingdom of God. Nicodemus saith unto him, How can a man be born when he is old? can he enter the second time into his mother's womb, and be born? Jesus answered, Verily, verily, I say unto thee, Except a man be born of water and of the Spirit, he cannot enter into the kingdom of God. That which is born of the flesh is flesh; and that which is born of the Spirit is spirit. Marvel not that I said unto thee, Ye must be born again. The wind bloweth where it listeth, and thou hearest the sound thereof, but canst not tell whence it cometh, and whither it goeth: so is every one that is born of the Spirit.
John 3:3-8

Until you confess and acknowledge the Lord Jesus as your savior, you will forever be subdued with trials and tribulation. Eternity is real, therefore if you are not a born again Christian, do so quickly before concluding this Holy Spirit-revealed manual.

THE FEAR OF GOD—
this is the beginning of wisdom

You must develop the consciousness of the fear of God in your heart if you desire to overcome trials and tribulations. As long as you fear God, the help of the Holy Spirit is on the way. "The Lord made it clear it shall be well with the righteous but it shall not be well with the wicked." (Ecclesiastes 8:12-13) "Though a sinner do evil an hundred times, and his days be prolonged, yet surely I know that it shall be well with them that fear God, which fear before him: But it shall not be well with the wicked, neither shall he prolong his days, which are as a shadow; because he feareth not before God." (Ecclesiastes 8:12-13) The Holy Spirit will choose you to teach you all things once you embrace the fear of God in your life. *"What man is he that feareth the Lord? him shall he teach in the way that he shall choose."* (Psalms 25:12)

RIGHTEOUS LIFESTYLE

Although righteousness is the platform to provoke the Holy Spirit, it is also the foundation to provoke the supernatural favor of God. *"He that diligently seeketh good procureth favour: but he that seeketh mischief, it shall come unto him."* (Proverbs 11:27) Righteousness, in my opinion, is the breathing ground for all around favor from God.

INTEGRITY

Every man/woman of integrity is a man/woman of favor. As long as you are morally and ethically right in all your affairs, false accusations may come—but you will prevail against it. This is a covenant promise sealed by the Holy Bible. *"Whoso keepeth the commandment shall feel no evil thing: and a wise man's heart discerneth both time and judgment."* (Ecclesiastes 8:5) It is written: *"And who is he that will harm you, if ye be followers of that which is good?"* (1 Peter 3:13)

Remember...

The integrity of the upright shall guide them: but the perverseness of transgressors shall destroy them.
Proverbs 11:30

SOUL WINNING

And Jesus came and spake unto them, saying, All power is given unto me in heaven and in earth. Go ye therefore, and teach all nations, baptizing them in the name of the Father, and of the Son, and of the Holy Ghost: Teaching them to observe all things whatsoever I have commanded you: and, lo, I am with you always, even unto the end of the world. Amen.
Matthew 28:18-20

In our lifetime we must be soul winners if we are to activate the power of the supernatural favor of God. It is written: *"All that the Father giveth me shall come to me; and him that cometh to me I will in no wise cast out."* (John 6:37) *"And he that winneth souls is wise."* (Proverbs 11:30)

OBEDIENCE

As long as you are walking in disobedience, you will never obtain the supernatural favor of God. *"If ye be willing and obedient, ye shall eat the good of the land: But if ye refuse and rebel, ye shall be devoured with the sword: for the mouth of the Lord hath spoken it."* (Isaiah 1:19-20)

PRAYER POINTS FOR THE HELP OF
THE HOLY SPIRIT

1) Father Lord, deliver me from this present trial, in the name of Jesus.

2) Almighty Father, bring me out of this present obscurity, in the name of Jesus.

3) Holy Spirit, help me to overcome this trial, in Jesus name.

4) Holy Spirit, speak to me, in the name of Jesus.

5) Holy Spirit, minister to my subconscious spirit, in the name of Jesus.

6) Fire of God, burn down every mountain of difficulty, in the name of Jesus.

7) Holy Ghost, baptize me with your fire, in the name of Jesus.

8) Holy Spirit, go before me and favor me in this present challenge, in the name of Jesus.

9) Spirit of God, grant me liberty and freedom by the fire of the Holy Spirit, in the name of Jesus.

10) Father Lord, intervene on my behalf, in the name of Jesus.

11) Ancient of day, liberate me this season, in the name of Jesus.

12) Immortal redeemer, bring me higher above these prevailing changes.

13) Lord God, turn this present obstacale into my miracle, in the name of Jesus.

14) Fire of God, break down these obstacles for me, in the name of Jesus.

15) Holy Spirit, favor me in, Jesus name.

16) Holy Spirit. release me from this challenge, in the name of Jesus.

17) Holy Spirit, become my compionion, in Jesus name.

18) Holy Spirit, represent me in this matter.

19) Holy Spirit, elevant me beyond my own immagination, in the name of Jesus.

20) Holy Spirit, do not allow my enemies to truimph over my life, in the name of Jesus.

21) Fire of God, protect me, in the name of Jesus.

22) Fire of God, destroy my enemies, in the name of Jesus.

23) Fire of God, build a wall around me, in the name of Jesus.

24) Fire of God, expose my enemies, in the name of Jesus.

25) Fire of God, prove yourself, in the name of Jesus.

26) Holy Spirit, represent me in jesus name.

27) Holy Spirit, release your boldnes into my life.

28) Holy Spirit, grant me signs and wonders.

29) Holy Spirit, make me a living wonder in my lifetime.

30) Holy Spirit, turn my life around, in the name of Jesus.

31) Holy Spirit, I will not remain at this level, in the name of Jesus.

32) Spirit of God, lift me higher, in the mighty name of Jesus.

33) Angels of God, minister unto me, in the name of Jesus.

34) Hand of God, separate me this season, in the name of Jesus.

CONCLUSION

Let us therefore come boldly unto the throne of grace, that we may obtain mercy, and find grace to help in time of need.
Hebrews 4:16

We must develop the habit to always go before the throne of mercy to find grace to help—especially in times of trouble. For us to walk in favor in our lifetime, we must always be humbled enough to seek the face of God, ask God *"for His mercy that endureth forever."* (Psalms 117:2) The reason David prevailed was because David knew the techniques for seeking the mercy of God anytime.

Let us hear the conclusion of the whole matter: Fear God, and keep his commandments: for this is the whole duty of man. For God shall bring every work into judgment, with every secret thing, whether it be good, or whether it be evil.
Ecclesiastes 12:13-14

All you have read remains a story until there is a transformation inside of your heart. The favor of God is provoked only when you FEAR GOD and keep HIS commandments. The Bible says: *"For God shall bring every work into judgment, with every secret thing, whether it be good, or whether it be evil."* (Ecclesiastes 12:14) If you are a born again Christian, we'd like to encourage you in your Christian life. If you are not a born again Christian, we can help you here receive genuine salvation. "Therefore if any man be in Christ, he is a new creature: old things are passed away; behold, all things are become new." (2 Corinthians 5:17)

Now repeat this prayer after me:

Say Lord Jesus, I accept you today, as my Lord and my savior, forgive me of my sins wash me with your blood. Right now, I believe, I am sanctified, I am save, I am free, I am free from the Power of sin to serve the Lord Jesus. Thank you Lord for saving me. Amen.

Congratulations: YOU ARE NOW A BORN AGAIN CHRISTIAN.

AGAIN I SAY TO YOU—CONGRATULATIONS!

What must I do to determine my divine visitation?

To determine divine visitation, you must be born again! The word says, *"As many as received Him, to them gave He power to become the sons of God. Even to them that believe on his name."* (John 1:12)

To qualify for divine visitation, do the following with sincerity—

> 1) Acknowledge that you are a sinner and that He died for you. (Romans 3:23)
> 2) Repent of your sins. (Acts 3:19, Luke 13:5,

2 Peter 3:9)
3) Believe in your heart that Jesus died for your sins. (Romans 10:10)
4) Confess Jesus as the Lord over your life. (Romans 10:10, Acts 2:21)

Now repeat this prayer after me:

Say Lord Jesus, I accept you today, as my Lord and my savior. Forgive me of my sins, wash me with your blood. Right now, I believe I am sanctified, I am saved, I am free. I am free from the power of sin, to serve the Lord Jesus. Thank you Lord for saving me. Amen.

Congratulations. You are now...

A BORN AGAIN CHRISTIAN.

Again I say to you—CONGRATULATIONS!

I adjure you to watch the Spirit of God bear witness with your Spirit, confirming His word with subsequent signs. The word says, *"The Spirit itself beareth witness with our spirit, that we are the children of God."* (Romans 8:16)

Join a bible believing church or join us on our weekly and Sunday worship services at 343 Sanford Avenue Newark New Jersey 07106.

WISDOM KEYS

— Every productive society is a society heading to the top.

— Millions of Nigerians run away from Nigeria. Very few Nigerians stay in Nigeria.

— My decision to return to Nigeria is the will of God for my life.

— My shortcoming in America after 18 years is the fact that I've trained myself to be wise, to think, reflect and reason appropriately.

— If you train your mind to reason, it will train your hands to earn money.

— It is absurd to use the money of the heathen to build the kingdom of the living God.

— Every ministry reveals its agenda and VISION either at the beginning or at the end.

— Be careful of your life. It is your first ministry.

— The average American mind is conditioned for a continual quest to get new things and discard the old.

— When I considered well, my BMW jeep became my

initial deposit for the work of the ministry in Nigeria.

—Money will never fall from any tree or person. Make up your mind to be independent today.

—Everyone is waiting for you to change your mind. Until you change your thinking, nothing changes around you.

—Multiple academic degrees in other disciplines gave me the chance to think and reason.

—Whatever anyone is thinking at any time reveals what is inside of their heart.

—All planned events are the product of meditation.

—Every event is designed for a designated timeline.

—Wisdom is your ability to think, to create and invent.

— If you can think wisely enough, you will come out of debt.

—The distance between you and your success is your innovative and creative ability to think well.

—Success is the result of hard work, commitment, resolve and determined learning from past mistakes and failings.

—If you organize your mind, you have organized your life and destiny.

—There is a thin line between success and failure.

—Wealth is your ability to think, power is your ability to reason and success is your ability to be informed.

—If you can make use of your mind by thinking and reasoning, God will make use of your life and destiny.

—Reflect, reason, think and be Great.

—Famous people are born of woman.

—That you will make it is your intention, that you will survive is your resolve, that you will succeed with changes is your determination, personal efforts and hard work.

—No man was born a failure.

—Lack of vision is the result of failure.

—Working with mental patients encourages and aspire me to be a productive observant and dedicated to my assignment.

—Successful people are not magicians. It is the will-power, combined with hard work and determination and a resolve to succeed, that make them succeed.

—In the unequivocal state of the mind, intention is not a location or a position. It is the state of the mind.

—So many people think that they think.

—The mind is used to think, to reflect and to reason.

—You will remain blind with your eyes open until you can see with your mind by thinking.

—There is no favoritism in accurate and precise calculation.

—Although knowledge is power, information is the key and gateway to a great future.

—It will take the hand of God to move the hand of man.

—With the backing of the great wise God, nothing will disconnect you from your inheritance.

—As long as you have wisdom and understanding of God, Satan and evil cannot manipulate your life and destiny.

—You have come this far in life by your own judgment and the decisions you made in the past. Now lean in and listen to God for another dimension of greatness.

—Great people are ordinary people. It is extra ordinary efforts and the price of sacrifice that produces greatness in them.

—As a mental direct care worker, I saw a great pastor and a motivational speaker within myself.

—A menial job does not reduce your self-worth. Until you resolve to achieve greatness and see greatness in all you do, you will never count in your community.

—The principle of Jesus will solve your gambling and addiction problems.

—The man of Jesus will lead you into heaven.

—Everyone has their self-appraisal and what they think about you. Until you discover yourself, other opinions about you will alter the real you.

—Supervisors and directors are just a position in the chain of command in a workplace. Never allow your supervisor hierarchy to alter your opinion of yourself.

—Everyone can come out of debt if they make up their mind.

—The fact that I am not a decision-maker at work does

not diminish my contribution to my world.

—Although it appears like it was a poor decision to accept a direct care employment at a psychiatric hospital, as I reflect on my nine years of that experience, it became apparent that I have learned and experienced enough for my next assignment.

—Self-encouragement and determination is a resolve of the heart.

—If you are determined to make a difference and do the things that make a difference, you will eventually make a difference.

—Good things do not come easy.

—Short cuts will cut your life short.

—Those who look ahead move ahead.

—Life is all about making an impact. In your lifetime strive to make an impact in your community.

—Make friends and connect with people who are moving ahead of you in life.

—If you can look around well, you have come a long way in your life, made a lot of difference and realized a lot of success in life.

—If you are my old friend, hurry up to reach out to me before I become a stranger to you.

—I am blessed with inspirations from God that changed my interpretation of the world around me.

—I thought I was stagnant and lonely until I looked around and noticed my children running around and my wife cooking.

— At 40, I resigned my job to seek the Lord forever.

—My ministry took a drastic rise to the top when the wisdom of God visited me with knowledge and understanding.

—You will be a better person if you understand the characteristics of your personality like your mood swings, attitudes and habits.

—It is the seed of love you sow into the heart of a child and a woman that you reap in due time.

—Love is not selfish. Love shares everything, including the concealed secrets of the mind.

—As long as you have a prayer life and a Bible, you will never feel lonely in the race of life.

—When good friends disconnect from you, let them

go. They might have seen something new in a different direction.

—Confidence in yourself and in God is the only way to bring you out of captivity

—Never train a child to waste his or her time.

—The mind is the greatest asset of a great future.

—You walk by common sense, run by principles and fly by instruction.

—Those who become successful in life did it by self-determination, hard work and learning from past failures.

—Most successful people are lonely people. No one renders help to them, believing they are already successful. Except when they seek for more knowledge and information, they are all alone.

— I have seen a towing truck vehicle. I have also seen a towing ship in the water. But I have never seen a towing airplane in the air.

—I exercise my judgment and make a decision every minute of the day. Decisions are crucial, critical and vital with reference to your future.

—So many people wish for a great future. You can

only work towards a great future.

—Your celebrity status began when you discovered your talent. What are you good at? Work at it with all your commitment.

—Prayers will sustain you, but the wisdom of God will prosper you.

—When I met Oyedepo, his teachings changed my perspective. But when I met Ibiyeomie, his teachings changed my perception.

— I will be successful in ministry if only I concentrate and focus my energy in the work of the ministry.

— It took the late Dr. Norman Vincent Peale's book to open my mind towards the kingdom of success.

CHAPTER 4
PRAYER OF SALVATION

I am glad you have read this book all the way from the beginning to this point. All I have said from the beginning will remain a mystery until you commit it into practice.

And before you do so, I want you—if you have not given your life to Jesus already—to do so now. Give your life to Christ. I want you to know the truth! The truth is that Jesus died for your sins and because He died, you must be alive and prosperous.

What must I do to determine my divine visitation?

To determine divine visitation, you must be born again! The word says, *"As many as received Him, to them gave He power to become the sons of God. Even to them that believe on his name."* (John 1:12)

To qualify for divine visitation, do the following with sincerity—

1) Acknowledge that you are a sinner and that He died for you. (Romans 3:23)
2) Repent of your sins. (Acts 3:19, Luke 13:5, 2 Peter 3:9)
3) Believe in your heart that Jesus died for your sins. (Romans 10:10)

4) Confess Jesus as the Lord over your life.
(Romans 10:10, Acts 2:21)

Now repeat this prayer after me:

Say Lord Jesus, I accept you today, as my Lord and my savior. Forgive me of my sins, wash me with your blood. Right now, I believe I am sanctified, I am saved, I am free. I am free from the power of sin, to serve the Lord Jesus. Thank you Lord for saving me. Amen.

Congratulations. You are now...

A BORN AGAIN CHRISTIAN.

Again I say to you—CONGRATULATIONS!

I adjure you to watch the Spirit of God bear witness with your Spirit, confirming His word with subsequent signs. The word says, *"The Spirit itself beareth witness with our spirit, that we are the children of God."* (Romans 8:16)

MIRACLE CARE OUTREACH

"...But that the members should have the same care one for another"
1 Corinthians 12:25

We are all members of the body of Christ. Jesus commanded us to love our neighbor as ourselves. This includes caring for one another as a member of one body. True love is expressed in caring and giving. The word says, for God so Love He gave....

Reach out to someone in need of Jesus. Help someone in crisis find Christ. Look out and prove your love to Jesus by caring and inviting your friends and associates to find Jesus the Healer.

Invite your friends to our Home Care Cell Fellowship (Miracle Chapel Intl. Satellite Fellowship). We're in the U.S. at 33 Schley Street, Newark, New Jersey 07112. Home Care Cell Fellowship Group meets every Tuesday at 6:00pm-7:00pm.

If you are in Nigeria—MIRACLE OF GOD MINISTRIES, a.k.a. "MIRACLE CHAPEL INTL." Mpama–Egbu-Owerri Imo state Nigeria.

LIFE IS NOT ALL ABOUT DURATION, BUT IT'S ALL ABOUT DONATION

What does this statement mean?

Life consists not in accumulation of material wealth. (Luke 12:15) But it's all about liberality...i.e., what you can give and share with others. (Proverbs

11:25) When you live for others, you live forever—because you outlive your generation by the legacy you leave behind after you depart into glory to be with the Lord. But when you live for yourself, when you are reduced to SELF—you are easily forgotten when you die and depart in glory.

Permit me to admonish you today to live your life to be a blessing to a soul connected to you today. I want you to know that so many souls are connected and looking up to you, and through you so many souls will be saved and rescued from destruction. Will you disciple someone today to find Jesus Christ?

As a genuine Christian, it is your duty to evangelize Jesus Christ to all you meet on your way. Jesus is still in the healing business—Jesus is still doing miracles, from time of old to now. Therefore, tell someone about Jesus Christ today, disciple and bring them to Church. "*Philip findeth Nathanael."* (John 1:45)

Please prove the sincerity of your love for God today, please become a soul winner. The dignity of your Christianity is hidden in your boldness to proclaim and evangelize Jesus Christ to all you meet on your way. There is a question mark on the integrity of your Christianity until you become a life soul winner. Invite someone to join us worship the Lord Jesus this coming Sunday. Amen.

MIRACLE OF GOD MINISTRIES
PILLARS OF THE COMMISSION

We Believe, Preach and Practice the following:

1) We believe and preach Salvation to every living human being.

2) We believe and preach Repentance and Forgiveness of sins.

3) We believe and preach the baptism of the Holy Spirit and Spiritual gifts.

4) We believe and teach Prosperity.

5) We believe and preach Divine Healing and Miracles—Signs and Wonder.

6) We believe and preach Faith.

7) We believe and proclaim the Power of God (Supernatural).

8) We believe and proclaim Praise and Worship to God.

9) We believe and preach Wisdom.

10) We believe and preach Holiness (Consecration).

11) We believe and preach Vision.

12) We believe and teach the Word of God.

13) We believe and teach Success.

14) We believe and practice Prayer.

15) We believe and teach Deliverance.

These 15 stones form the Pillars of Our Commission.
Become part of this church family and follow this great move of God.

MY HEART FELT PRAYER FOR YOU

Our mission is simply to bring word of healing from the revelation of God word. I pray you will get into contact with many more of our books and materials. Remain blessed in the Mighty Name of Jesus Christ. I love to hear you feedback and letter. I also long to hear of your testimonies. Do not hesitate to contact us quickly.

NOW LET ME PRAY FOR YOU—
Father Lord by the intercession of the Holy Spirit, I ask for you today to reveal yourself and manifest your agenda over this life of this precious soul. May they provoke your unmerited favor the remaining days of their lives in the mighty name of Jesus. Thank you, Jesus, for hearing us together.
AMEN.

PROVOKING THE FAVOR OF GOD

If truly you desire the favor of God in your life, you must do what attracts it into your life. Do not be stingy and selfish, especially when you have the privilege and it is in your power to help someone around you. God does not like such a selfish attitude. It withdraws the favor of God from your life. It is written: *"Withhold not good from them to whom it is due, when it is in the power of thine hand to do it. Say not unto thy neighbour, Go, and come again, and tomorrow I will give; when thou hast it by thee."* (Proverbs 3:27-28) If you love God, you must love His kingdom and His righteousness.

DO YOU PAY YOUR TITHES?

"Will a man rob God? Yet ye have robbed me. But ye say, Wherein have we robbed thee? In tithes and offerings. Ye are cursed with a curse: for ye have robbed me, even this whole nation. Bring ye all the tithes into the storehouse, that there may be meat in mine house, and prove me now herewith, saith the Lord of hosts, if I will not open you the windows of heaven, and pour you out a blessing, that there shall not be room enough to receive it." (Malachi 3:8-10)

Make a commitment to join a Bible-believing church, worship the Lord Jesus every Sunday and pay your tithes so that things will not be thither for you. Jesus said, *"Freely ye have received, freely give."* (Matthew 10:8)

ABOUT THE AUTHOR

Rev. Franklin N. Abazie is the founding and Presiding Pastor of Miracle of God Ministries, with headquarters in Newark, New Jersey USA and a branch church in Owerri-Imo State Nigeria. He is following the footsteps of one of his mentors, the healing evangelist Oral Roberts of the blessed memory. The Lord passed Oral Roberts' healing mantle two days before he went to be with the Lord at age 91 into the hands of healing evangelist Rev. Franklin N. Abazie in a vision.

In all his services, the Power and Presence of God is present to heal all in his audience. Rev. Abazie is an ordained man of God, with a Healing Ministry reviving the healing and miracle ministry of Jesus Christ of Nazareth.

Pastor Franklin N. Abazie, has been called by God with a unique mandate: **"THE MOMENT IS DUE TO IMPACT YOUR WORLD THROUGH THE REVIVAL OF THE HEALING AND MIRACLE MINISTRY OF JESUS CHRIST OF NAZARETH.**

"I AM SENDING YOU TO RESTORE HEALTH UNTO THEE AND I WILL HEAL THEE OF THY WOUNDS, SAID THE LORD OF HOST."

Rev. Abazie is a gifted, ardent teacher of the word of God, who operates also in the office of a

Prophet, generating and attracting undeniable signs and wonders, special miracles and healings, with apostolic fireworks of the Holy Ghost. He is the founding and presiding senior Pastor of this fast growing Healing Ministry. He has written over 86 inspirational, healing and transforming books covering almost all aspects of divine healing and life. He is happily married and blessed with children.

BOOKS BY REV. FRANKLIN N. ABAZIE:

1) The Outcome of Faith
2) Understanding the Secret of Prevailing Prayers
3) Commanding Abundance
4) Understanding the Secret of the Man God Uses
5) Activating My Due Season
6) Overcoming Divine Verdicts
7) The Outcome of Divine Wisdom
8) Understanding God's Restoration Mandate
9) Walking In the Victory and Authority of the Truth
10) God's Covenant Exemption
11) Destiny Restoration Pillars
12) Provoking Acceptable Praise
13) Understanding Divine Judgment
14) Activating Angelic Re-enforcement
15) Provoking Un-Merited Favo
16) The Benefits of the Speaking Faith
17) Understanding Divine Arrangement
18) How to Keep Your Healing
19) Understanding the Mysteries of the Speaking Faith
20) Understanding the Mysteries of Prophetic Healing
21) Operating Under the Rules of Creative Healing
22) Understanding the Joy of Breakthrough
23) Understanding the Mystery of Breakthrough
24) Understanding Divine Prosperity
25) Understanding Divine Healing
26) Retaining Your Inheritance
27) Overcoming Confusing Spirit
28) Commanding Angelic Escorts

29) Enforcing Your Inheritance In Christ Jesus
30) Understanding Your Guardian Angels
31) Overcoming the Dominion of Sin
32) Understanding the Voice of God
33) The Outstanding Benefits of the Anointing
34) The Audacity of the Blood of Jesus
35) Walking in the Reality of the Anointing
36) Escaping the Nightmare of Poverty
37) Understanding Your Harvest Season
38) Activating Your Success Buttons
39) Overcoming the Forces of Darkness
40) Overcoming the Devices of the Devil
41) Overcoming Demonic Agents
42) Overcoming the Sorrows of Failure
43) Rejecting the Sorrows of Failure
44) Resisting the Sorrows of Poverty
45) Restoring Broken Marriages
46) Redeeming Your Days
47) The Force of Vision
48) Overcoming the Forces of Ignorance
49) Understanding the Sacrifice of Small Beginning
50) The Might of Small Beginning
51) Understanding the Mysteries of Prophesy
52) Overcoming Dream Nightmares
53) Breaking the Shackles of the Curse of the Law
54) Understanding the Joy of Harvest
55) Wisdom for Signs & Wonders
56) Wisdom for Generational Impact
57) Wisdom for Marriage Stability
58) Understanding the Number of Your Days

59) Enforcing Your Kingdom Rights
60) Escaping the Traps of Immoralities
61) Escaping the Trap of Poverty
62) Accessing Biblical Prosperity
63) Accessing True Riches in Christ
64) Silencing the Voice of the Accuser
65) Overcoming the Forces of Oppositions
66) Quenching the Voice of the Avenger
67) Silencing Demonic Prediction & Projection
68) Silencing Your Mocker
69) Understanding the Power of the Holy Ghost
70) Understanding the Baptism of Power
71) The Mystery of the Blood of Jesus
72) Understanding the Mystery of Sanctification
73) Understanding the Power of Holiness
74) Understanding the Forces of Purity & Righteousness
75) Activating the Forces of Vengeance
76) Appreciating the Mystery of Restoration
77) Overcoming the Projection & Prediction of the Enemy
78) Engaging the Mystery of the Blood
79) Commanding the Power of the Speaking Faith
80) Uprooting the Forces Against Your Rising
81) Overcoming Mere Success Syndrome
82) Understanding Divine Sentence
83) Understanding the Mystery of Praise
84) Understanding the Author of Faith
85) The Mystery of the Finisher of Faith
86) Attracting Supernatural Favor

MIRACLE OF GOD MINISTRIES
NIGERIA CRUSADE
2012

MIRACLE OF GOD MINISTRIES
NIGERIA CRUSADE 2012

MIRACLE OF GOD MINISTRIES

NIGERIA CRUSADE

2012

MIRACLE OF GOD MINISTRIES

NIGERIA CRUSADE

2012

MIRACLE OF GOD MINISTRIES

NIGERIA CRUSADE 2012

www.ingramcontent.com/pod-product-compliance
Lightning Source LLC
Chambersburg PA
CBHW021449080526
44588CB00009B/765